300
calories
or less!

300 calories or less!

Delicious recipes for just **300** calories or less

First published in 2012
LOVE FOOD is an imprint of Parragon Books Ltd

Parragon
Queen Street House
4 Queen Street
Bath BA1 1HE, UK

www.parragon.com/lovefood

ISBN: 978-1-4454-9864-5
Printed in China

New recipes and introduction by Robin Donovan
New photography by Clive Streeter
Home economy for new photography by Teresa Goldfinch
Nutritional analysis by Fiona Hunter

Notes for the Reader

This book uses both metric and imperial measurements. Follow the same units of measurement throughout; do not mix metric and imperial. All spoon measurements are level: teaspoons are assumed to be 5 ml, and tablespoons are assumed to be 15 ml. Unless otherwise stated, milk is assumed to be full fat, eggs and individual vegetables are medium, and pepper is freshly ground black pepper. Unless otherwise stated, all root vegetables should be washed in plain water and peeled prior to using. For best results, use a food thermometer when cooking meat and poultry – check the latest government guidelines for current advice.

Garnishes, decorations and serving suggestions are all optional and not necessarily included in the recipe ingredients or method. Any optional ingredients and seasoning to taste are not included in the nutritional analysis. Nutritional analysis is per serving (Serves ...) or per item (Makes ...). The times given are an approximate guide only. Preparation times differ according to the techniques used by different people and the cooking times may also vary from those given. Optional ingredients, variations or serving suggestions have not been included in the time calculations.

Recipes using raw or very lightly cooked eggs should be avoided by infants, the elderly, pregnant women, convalescents and anyone suffering from an illness. Pregnant and breastfeeding women are advised to avoid eating peanuts and peanut products. Sufferers from nut allergies should be aware that some of the ready-made ingredients used in the recipes in this book may contain nuts. Always check the packaging before use. Vegetarians should be aware that some of the ready-made ingredients used in the recipes in this book may contain animal products. Always check the packaging before use.

Picture acknowledgements

Front cover: Two fresh tomatoes with vine © Jill Fromer/Getty Images and Broccoli on White Background © Lilli Day/Getty Images.

Contents

Finally, a Low-Calorie Diet Made Easy – And Delicious!

You've heard it before, but few factors have such a profound effect on our health than our weight. Achieving or maintaining a healthy weight may just be the best thing you can do for yourself. Not just for your appearance, but for every aspect of your life. You may like the way you look better, but far more importantly, you'll feel better, have more energy, get sick less often and be less likely to develop weight-related diseases such as hypertension and diabetes – and you'll more likely live longer too.

While losing weight is never easy, the fact is that for most of us it's not rocket science. Actually, it's just plain and simple maths: calories in versus calories out. Eat the same number of calories you burn to maintain weight, eat fewer than you burn to lose weight.

But, you groan, counting calories is a hassle, isn't it? It takes dedication, patience, time and commitment. Reading every label and looking up every ingredient is so dull! Plus, there is the dreaded sense that you have to

give up all your favourite foods. If all of that makes you want to toss in the towel before you've even started, I don't blame you.

However, there is good news! Losing or maintaining your weight by sticking to a low-calorie diet doesn't have to be difficult, or even unpleasant. Choosing healthy foods – foods that are packed with nutrients instead of added fat, sugar and other empty calories – can be just as easy as stuffing yourself with junk. And, believe it or not, it can be just as enjoyable too. The trick is making sure that healthy, low-calorie foods are just as readily available and easy to prepare as the high-calorie foods you're accustomed to eating.

Alas, many of us are so used to grabbing convenient but unhealthy snacks on the go that we've forgotten just what a healthy diet is. Here's an easy way to remember it: fresh, whole, unprocessed fruit and veggies, lean proteins (pulses, tofu, white poultry meat, fish and even lean cuts of pork or other red meats), nuts, and wholegrains are good; highly processed foods – or foods with long lists of ingredients (especially added sugars or fats) – and fried foods are bad. Simple!

How to Use This Book

The book you are holding in your hands is a great resource because it provides recipes that have been developed, tested and analysed to ensure that the dishes they produce are not only delicious but are also low in calories. As the title suggests, every dish in this book contains 300 calories or less.

You can mix and match the recipes to come up with a complete meal plan – including breakfast, lunch, dinner, snacks and desserts – made up of foods you love. Whether you are trying to lose weight or to simply maintain your current weight, you can easily stick to your calorie limit without having to count a thing.

For the average person trying to lose weight, nutritionists recommend a daily calorie limit of 1,200 to 1,500 calories for women and 1,500 to 2,000 calories for men. If you are hoping to simply maintain your weight, 1,800 to 2,200 calories may work for you.

Using those guidelines, you can enjoy four to six dishes from the recipes in this book each day. If you're sticking to the lower calorie limit, for instance, you can enjoy breakfast, lunch, dinner and a snack. For the middle and higher end of the range, you might add another snack and/or a dessert (just don't forget to count any drinks, such as juice or milk, when calculating your day's totals).

Fill your storecupboards with wholesome treats and snacks (we'll give you some ideas!) and try out a few quick and easy recipes such as the ones in this book, and you may be surprised by how easy it is to stick to a healthy diet.

What *Should* You Weigh?

Right about now, you may be wondering, 'Hmmm, what IS a healthy weight for me, anyway?' The best way to work that out is to look at your Body Mass Index, or BMI, which is a fancy name for a number that refers to your weight in relation to your height.

Assuming you know how tall you are, you can calculate your BMI with a simple formula: your weight in kilograms divided by your height in metres squared – Weight (kg)/ Height (m)^2.

For instance, a 1.65-metre tall person who weighs 64 kilograms would have a BMI of 23.5, which is within the healthy range.

Here's a formula for imperial measurements: your weight in pounds divided by your height in inches squared, times by 703 – Weight (lb)/ Height (inches)^2 x 703.

Using imperial measurements (remember there are 14 pounds to 1 stone): a person who is 5 feet, 5 inches tall (65 inches) and weighs 10 stone, so 140 pounds, would have a BMI of 23.3:

$140/65^2 \times 703 = 23.3$ or ...

$65 \times 65 = 4{,}225; 140 \div 4{,}225 = 0.033136; 0.033136 \times 703 = 23.3$ (rounded off)

A healthy weight person will have a BMI between 18.5 and 24.9. If you are within this range, congratulations! While you may want to adopt healthier eating habits, you don't have a weight problem, so you don't need to worry about losing weight. However, if your BMI is 25 or higher, you can use this book to overhaul your diet and achieve a healthier weight.

Setting a goal weight can be tricky. There is a temptation to shoot for the moon, so to speak, and set a goal that would put your BMI at a svelte 18.5, but if you're starting out, say, in the high 20s, be careful about setting yourself up for disappointment and failure. Try setting an easier goal to start. For instance, you might set a goal that would bring your BMI down to 27. Once you've achieved that weight and maintained it for a while, you can re-evaluate and, with that success under your belt, set a new goal that brings your BMI down to, say, 24.

Further, if your goal is to lose weight, don't try to lose it too fast. You'll have longer lasting success if you lose around two pounds, or about a kilogram, per week. While fad diets and starvation may help you shed weight fast, you'll be likely to gain the weight again the minute you go back to eating normally. Far better is a diet plan that helps you develop healthier habits that you can maintain for the long haul. This book will help you learn how to choose healthier alternatives for many of your favourite foods. Stick with it for a month or two, and you'll likely find that you begin to prefer the healthier options as you'll feel better and will be more energetic, less sluggish and healthier.

And rest assured, no one is expecting you to be a saint. Go ahead and cheat every once in a while. If you find your mother's cheesecake simply irresistible, go ahead and indulge in a slice (or two!) the next time you visit. If buttered popcorn brings you incomparable joy when you go to the cinema, let yourself live a little now and then. What's more important is that you make healthy choices in your everyday life. Keeping your storecupboard stocked with wholesome, nutritious foods and learning to prepare healthy meals

will give you the tools you need to achieve or maintain a healthy weight.

If your goal is to lose weight, plan to eat around 1,200 to 1,500 calories per day for women or 1,500 to 2,000 calories for men. If your goal is to maintain your weight, 1,800 to 2,200 calories per day should be fine. This book makes that easy because every recipe in it contains 300 calories or less per serving, making it simple to mix and match for a balanced diet that is within your allowed calorie range. For instance, you might choose one breakfast dish, one lunch dish, one dinner dish, a snack and, if you're feeling indulgent, a dessert. But don't let the categories limit you. There's nothing wrong with having breakfast for dinner or dinner for lunch! The most important thing is eating a range of nutritious foods (and sorry, eating five puddings a day is not okay, even if it would be within the calorie limits!).

Watch Your Portions

In addition to choosing healthy foods, it's important to pay attention to portion sizes. A small bowl of pasta is perfectly acceptable, but keep an eye on the amount you are giving yourself:

- A portion of meat is about 85 g/3 oz
- A portion of white fish is about 175 g/6 oz
- A portion of sliced sandwich meat is about 85 g/3 oz
- A portion of cheese is about 25 g/1 oz
- A portion of mashed potatoes is about 200 g/7 oz
- A portion of hot cooked rice is about 200 g/7 oz
- A portion of ice cream is 1 scoop, about 70 g/2 oz
- A portion of fruit is about the size of a small fist

Mindful Eating

One of the best practices to help keep you on track is just to pay attention when you are eating. Instead of watching television or checking your emails while you eat, really focus on your food – and you'll not only be likely to eat less but you'll enjoy your food more.

It takes about 20 minutes for your brain to get a message from your stomach saying it is satisfied. As a result eating slowly will also help to prevent over-eating as it will give your stomach a chance to send the message to your brain that it has had enough before you over-indulge.

Keeping a Food Tracker

If you have a tendency to eat mindlessly or simply eat the foods and quantities you do out of habit, a food tracker will be an extremely useful tool. By learning to pay attention to every morsel of food that passes your lips you'll learn lots about when, why and what you eat.

You'll likely be surprised by some of the things you'll learn. Just by increasing your awareness of your eating habits, you'll find changing them to be much easier. Perhaps you don't even realize that you always put a double serving of cream cheese on your morning bagel or eat half the bag of crisps that supposedly contains five servings.

Take your food tracker with you wherever you go and use it to record every single thing you eat. Do this for at least a full week, or ideally a month.

To make your food tracker as useful as possible, include details about what, when and how much you eat. For instance, '6 pm: 3 slices of veggie pizza with extra cheese in the car on the way home' is a more useful entry than simply 'pizza'. To really make the tracker useful, consider including other details such as what you were doing while you ate (watching television, reading, driving, chatting with a friend), as well as how you were feeling (sad, happy, stressed out) at the time.

All of this information will help you identify the times that you are likely to over-eat or any emotional cues that trigger poor eating habits. It will also help you to compensate for indulgences. For instance, if you eat a bacon cheeseburger for lunch one day, you can make up for it by having a salad with low-fat dressing the next.

Keeping track of the times you eat can also help you to regulate your appetite. Eating meals and snacks at regular intervals throughout the day will keep you from ever becoming ravenous – a sure set-up for bingeing on unhealthy foods.

What is a Healthy Diet?

How much and how often you eat are important but of course you can't overlook the significance of what you eat. Specifically, a healthy diet includes lots of fresh fruits and vegetables, lean proteins such as pulses, tofu, fish and shellfish, skinless white poultry meat and nuts, and wholegrains such as brown rice, wholemeal breads and quinoa.

A healthy plate looks something like this:

Fill half of your plate with fresh vegetables and fruits, one quarter with wholegrains such as brown rice or quinoa, and the other quarter with lean protein such as fish, pulses, tofu or skinless chicken breast.

It's About What You Can Eat, Not What You Can't

Instead of thinking of a healthy diet as one of deprivation, think instead of all the delicious and wholesome foods you can eat. In fact the more variety in your diet the better, as this helps to ensure that you get all of the necessary nutrients including vitamins, minerals, fibre, protein, healthy fats and complex carbohydrates. Eating a range of foods also limits your risk of over-exposure to toxic chemicals such as pesticides that may be present in certain foods.

Eating a rainbow of fruits and vegetables – orange citrus and melon, yellow pineapple, green apples, red peppers and tomatoes, purple aubergines and blueberries for instance – keeps your meals interesting and also provides you with a wide range of vitamins and other nutrients.

High-fibre foods including fresh fruits, vegetables, pulses and wholegrains are packed with nutrients and are relatively low in calories, making them great candidates for satisfying hunger. Fibre also keeps you feeling fuller for longer, so you won't be tempted to over-eat between meals.

Why Wholegrains?

Wholegrains are unrefined grains that contain the entire grain kernel. Refined grains, on the other hand, have been milled to remove the bran and germ, giving them a more palatable texture but also stripping them of vital nutrients such as iron, fibre and the B vitamins. In a healthy diet at least half of the grains or grain products consumed should be wholegrains.

Healthy Fats

Healthy fats – the monounsaturated fats such as those from rapeseed oil or olive oil, avocadoes and nuts – provide important nutrients and help with the absorption of many vitamins. These fats are a crucial part of a healthy diet. Solid fats such as butter, lard and other animal fat, white vegetable fat and hydrogenated vegetable oils are high in saturated fat, cholesterol and trans fat and should be avoided as much as possible.

Read the Fine Print!

In order to maintain a healthy diet while juggling our fast-paced lives, many of us have no choice but to rely on ready-prepared or convenience foods. Don't worry, however – those foods aren't off-limits. In fact these days the ready-prepared foods aisle in the supermarket has lots of healthy options. You just need to know how to recognize them. That's where reading nutrition labels comes in. These labels contain copious information including how many calories are in each serving of the food and, equally important, how many servings are in the packet. You'll also find valuable information about the food's cholesterol, fat, protein, fibre and salt content. See below for a breakdown of daily requirements.

Calories and other values	Grams/day for 1,500-calorie diet	Grams/day for 1,200-calorie diet
30–35% of cal. from fat*	50–60g	40–45g
15–20% of cal. from protein	45–60g	35–50g
45–65% of cal. from carbs	135–195g	110–155g
Fibre	25g	20g
Salt	<6g	<6g
Saturated fat	<18g	<15g

* The majority of the fat in your diet, 20 to 25 per cent of total calories, should be unsaturated with the remaining 10 to 15 per cent saturated. Trans fats should be avoided.

Get Moving!

Wouldn't it be wonderful if we could all look and feel fantastic without any work? Well, dream on! Looking and feeling your best requires effort. Not only do you have to make good food choices, but you'll also need to participate in regular physical activity.

But wait – before you get your knickers in a twist, take comfort in the fact that you don't have to devote hours of each day to sweating it out at the gym. In fact just adding a few 10-minute bursts of activity throughout your day may be enough to rev your metabolism so you'll burn more calories, lose weight and, better yet, look and feel your best.

Walking is one of the easiest ways to work more activity into your day-to-day routines. You can start out by simply walking around the neighbourhood at a brisk pace at lunchtime, or even parking a couple of streets away from work rather than right in front. Take the stairs instead of the lift, walk to do your errands rather than drive or get a work colleague to join you for a lunchtime stroll (and gossip session!).

Other daily activities can serve as exercise too. Even chores such as housework and gardening will get your blood pumping if you approach them with enthusiasm.

People who are very social often enjoy participating in exercise classes, dance lessons or sports clubs. If you're a person who likes taking risks or are a nature lover, rock climbing, trekking or mountain biking may be just your cup of tea. Walking, running and yoga are good options for people who crave time to be alone with their thoughts.

The following chart shows the per hour calories burnt for a wide range of activities.

Physical Activity	Calories/Hour*
Stretching	180
Weight lifting (light workout)	220
Walking (3½ mph)	280
Bicycling (<10 mph)	290
Light gardening/garden work	330
Dancing	330
Golf (walking and carrying clubs)	330
Trekking	370
Heavy garden work (chopping wood)	440
Weight lifting (vigorous effort)	440
Basketball (vigorous)	440
Walking (4½ mph)	460
Aerobics	480
Swimming (slow freestyle laps)	510
Running/jogging (5 mph)	590
Bicycling (>10 mph)	590

*Calories per hour for 70-kg/11-stone person

No time for exercise? Try working these activities into your day:

- Walk or bike to work, school or the shops instead of driving
- Park your car or get off the bus a few streets from your destination
- Take the stairs instead of the lift
- Spend 10 minutes stretching at your desk
- Walk around the local area instead of just going to the canteen or break room at work
- Play a chasing game with your children before dinner
- Take your dog to a neighbourhood park for a game of fetch
- Mow the lawn, rake the leaves or do some weeding in the garden
- Use hand weights or an exercise band, or do sit-ups or press-ups while you watch television

Once you find an activity you enjoy, make a commitment to do it regularly (three to five times per week) for a minimum of 30 days. By the end of that time it's more than likely that your new routine will have become such a habit that you won't be able to imagine giving it up.

How Much Exercise Do You Need?

Ideally every single one of us should be participating in a minimum of 30 to 60 minutes of moderate to intense physical activity every day, but while lots is better than a little, a little is certainly better than none. Start out doing as much as you can each day and then increase the amount of time by a few minutes each day.

Shopping for a Healthy Diet

When trying to stick to a healthy diet, the supermarket can be a minefield, full of enticing – and off-limits – treats that are like ticking time bombs, poised to blow all of your good intentions out of the water.

Fresh foods are usually found around the perimeter of the supermarket, so try to stick to these areas as much as possible, loading your trolley with fresh fruits, veggies, lean proteins and the like. Duck into the centre aisles only when needed, say, for a loaf of wholemeal bread, some guilt-free condiments such as mustard and vinegar, or the occasional healthy treat such as frozen yogurt.

Stock up on snack foods and other items that are easy to grab and prepare and that are packed with nutrition rather than fat, sugar or calories. These include fresh fruits and veggies as well as wholegrain savoury biscuits, low-fat dairy foods, nuts and seeds, and dried fruits.

On the Go Healthy Snack Foods

• Fresh fruits (apples, berries, oranges, pineapple, bananas)
• Fresh vegetables (especially baby carrots, celery, peppers, cherry tomatoes and other veggies that can be eaten raw with minimal prep)

- Dried fruits
- Nuts
- Wholegrain savoury biscuits
- Low-fat dairy foods (yogurt, skimmed milk, reduced-fat cheeses)
- Wholegrain or high-fibre, low-sugar cereals

- Sweet treats (sweeties, chocolate bars, biscuits, ice cream)
- Fizzy drinks and squash

Storecupboard Standbys for Quick-and-Easy Meals

- Wholewheat pasta
- Brown rice
- Quinoa
- Canned beans (black, borlotti, cannellini, chickpea, pinto)
- Winter greens (chard, kale, cabbage)
- Salad leaves (lettuce, baby spinach, rocket)
- Squashes (acorn, butternut, courgettes) and pumpkins
- Sweet potatoes or yams
- Tofu
- Skinless chicken breasts
- Pork fillet
- Fish or shellfish

Foods to Steer Your Trolley Clear Of

- Full-fat dairy products
- Fatty meats
- White breads
- White rice
- High-sugar cereals

Tips for Easy, Healthy Cooking

Cooking for yourself is the best way to ensure that the food you eat is full of beneficial nutrients and light on fat and empty calories. Here are a few tips to take into the kitchen. Follow them to lighten up your dishes without losing the taste factor.

Add Flavour Without Adding Calories

Dishes don't have to be high in calories to be delicious. Rather than adding flavour by using high-fat options such as butter or cheese, choose healthier, low-fat ingredients such as the ones listed below to add plenty of flavour without the calories.

- Aromatics such as garlic, onions and fresh ginger
- Mustard
- Horseradish
- Citrus juice and zest
- Hot sauce or salsa
- Fresh, dried or pickled chillies
- Capers
- Gherkins, pickled vegetables or pickle relish
- Dried spices (cayenne, chilli powder, cumin, cinnamon, etc.)
- Fresh or dried herbs (thyme, oregano, basil, rosemary, dill, etc.)

- Vinegar (wine, balsamic or flavoured with herbs or fruit)

Choose Your Cooking Fat Wisely

One of the easiest ways to cut calories and saturated fat from your home cooking is to reduce the amount and/or change the type of fat that you use to cook. Many recipes will call for, say, 25 g/1 oz of butter when just a little splash of vegetable oil would do the job just as well. Not only are you using less of the fat this way but, unlike butter, vegetable oil contains less saturated fat or cholesterol.

Get yourself a can of olive, sunflower or vegetable oil spray and use it to coat your frying pans with a thin film of oil whenever a recipe calls for sautéing in oil. This spray can also be used to coat baking tins for baking or to coat vegetables for roasting.

Choose Your Cooking Method Wisely

We all know that veggies are good for us, but you can over-ride nearly all of a vegetable's health benefits by choosing the wrong cooking method. For instance, courgettes are low in calories but high in a host of beneficial nutrients including vitamin C and potassium. Coat courgettes in batter and deep-fry

them and suddenly they are a fat-and-calorie bomb. Steaming, roasting and light sautéing are far better options for cooking vegetables.

The Sweet Stuff

Refined sugar provides empty calories. In other words all you get for those calories are extra pounds without any extra nutrients. Fruits and fruit juices are great substitutes as they provide sweetness to dishes with fewer added calories and more additional nutrients. Fruits and fruit purées such as apple purée can be used in both savoury and sweet sauces, as well as in baked goods. Try replacing half of the sugar in your favourite cake or muffin recipe with apple purée and you will find that the result is even more moist and delicious than normal.

Sample One-Week Meal Plan

Monday:
Breakfast: Apple Spice Oats
Lunch: Chicken & Spicy Peanut Salad
Dinner: Spaghetti with Bacon-Tomato Sauce
Snack/Dessert: Caramel Popcorn Bites

Tuesday:
Breakfast: Cherry Almond Granola
Lunch: Falafel Pitta Parcels
Dinner: White Chicken Chilli
Snack/Dessert: Pear & Blueberry Strudel

Wednesday:
Breakfast: Berry Rhubarb Muffins
Lunch: Prawn Taco Salad
Dinner: Spicy Sweetcorn Chowder
Snack/Dessert: Buttermilk Brownies

Thursday:
Breakfast: Berry Sunrise Smoothie
Lunch: Turkey-Avocado & BLT Wrap
Dinner: Chicken & Vegetable Enchiladas
Snack/Dessert: Maple-Nut Granola Bars

Friday:
Breakfast: Crustless Sweetcorn &
Cheddar Quiche
Lunch: Tomato & Feta Salad
Dinner: Prawn & Sausage Jambalaya
Snack/Dessert: Apple-Berry Crumble

Saturday:
Breakfast: Pumpkin Pecan Pancakes
Lunch: Crab Salad Sandwiches
Dinner: Broccoli Pizza
Snack/Dessert: Chocolate Soufflés

Sunday:
Breakfast: Poached Eggs in Tomato Sauce
Lunch: Roasted Vegetable Melts
Dinner: Halibut with Romesco Sauce
Snack/Dessert: Mini Pumpkin Cheesecakes

Chapter 1
Breakfast

apple spice oats

Vegetarian

Calories: 300   Fat: 8g   Sat Fat: 3g   Salt: 0.7g   Carb: 27.5g

Cook: 25 min   Prep: 10 min

Serves 6

2 sprays of vegetable oil spray

2 large eggs

150 ml/5 fl oz skimmed milk

50 g/1¾ oz soft light brown sugar

120 g/4 oz apple sauce

1 tsp baking powder

½ tsp salt

¼ tsp ground cinnamon

220 g/8 oz porridge oats

2 large, red-skinned apples, cored and diced

70 g/2½ oz dried fruit (raisins, apricots, cranberries, cherries or a combination)

1 tbsp unsalted butter, melted

1 Preheat the oven to 190°C/375°F/Gas Mark 5. Coat a shallow, wide ovenproof dish or 6 x 225-ml/8-fl-oz ramekins with vegetable oil spray.

2 Beat the eggs and milk in a bowl. Add the brown sugar, apple sauce, baking powder, salt and cinnamon and stir until thoroughly mixed. Stir in the oats, apples and dried fruit and mix well.

3 Spoon the mixture into the prepared ovenproof dish (or ramekins), add dots of the butter, and bake in the preheated oven for about 25 minutes or until hot and bubbling.

cherry almond granola

Vegan

Calories: 242   **Fat:** 11g   **Sat Fat:** 3.5g   **Salt:** 0.1g   **Carb:** 16g
Cook: 1¼ hr   **Prep:** 15 min

Serves 10

1 spray of vegetable oil spray

220 g/8 oz porridge oats

50 g/1¾ oz desiccated coconut

50 g/1¾ oz flaked almonds

55 g/2 oz ground linseeds

¼ tsp salt

120 ml/4 fl oz maple syrup

4 tbsp water

1 tbsp vegetable oil

1 tsp vanilla extract

100 g/3½ oz stoned dried cherries, chopped

1 Preheat the oven to 140°C/275°F/Gas Mark 1. Line a large baking tray with baking paper and spray it lightly with the vegetable oil spray.

2 In a large bowl, combine the oats, coconut, almonds, linseeds and salt and stir to mix well. In a small bowl, combine the maple syrup, water, vegetable oil and vanilla extract. Pour the liquid mixture over the dry mixture and stir well. Pour the mixture on to the prepared baking tray and spread out into an even layer.

3 Bake in the preheated oven for about 45 minutes, then stir well and spread out again into an even layer. Continue to bake for a further 30–40 minutes until crisp and beginning to colour. Stir in the cherries and leave to cool to room temperature.

4 Store in a tightly covered container at room temperature for up to a week.

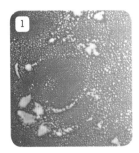

blueberry & honey yogurt

 Vegetarian

 Quick & Easy

Calories: 215   **Fat:** 11g   **Sat Fat:** 2g   **Salt:** Trace   **Carb:** 18g

Cook: 5 min   **Prep:** 15 min

Serves 4

3 tbsp clear honey

100 g/3½ oz mixed unsalted nuts

115 g/4 oz reduced-fat Greek-style yogurt

225 g/8 oz fresh blueberries

1 Heat the honey in a small saucepan over a medium heat. Add the nuts and stir until they are well coated. Remove from the heat and leave to cool slightly.

2 Divide the yogurt between four serving bowls, then spoon the nut mixture over the yogurt, top with the blueberries and serve immediately.

berry rhubarb muffins

Calories: 300   Fat: 9.5g   Sat Fat: 4g   Salt: 0.7g   Carb: 52g
Cook: 20–25 min   Prep: 15 min plus cooling

Makes 12

1 spray of vegetable oil spray

155 g/5½ oz plain flour

140 g/5 oz wholemeal flour

30 g/1 oz ground linseeds

1 tsp baking powder

1 tsp bicarbonate of soda

55 g/2 oz unsalted butter, softened

220 g/8 oz sugar

100 g/3½ oz soft light brown sugar

235 ml/8½ fl oz semi-skimmed buttermilk

1 egg

1 tsp vanilla extract

125 g/4½ oz rhubarb, finely diced

160 g/5¾ oz strawberries, diced

salt

Crumble topping

15 g/½ oz unsalted butter

2 tbsp plain flour

2 tbsp soft light brown sugar

2 tsp ground linseeds

2 tbsp pecan nut pieces

1 Preheat the oven to 200°C/400°F/Gas Mark 6. Spray a 12-hole muffin tin with vegetable oil spray.

2 To make the muffin mixture, combine the flours, linseeds, baking powder, bicarbonate of soda, and ½ teaspoon of salt in a medium bowl and stir well. In a large bowl, cream the butter and sugars together with an electric whisk. Add the buttermilk, egg and vanilla extract to the butter-sugar mixture and beat on medium–high speed until well combined. Add the flour mixture in three batches, beating on medium speed after each addition until just incorporated. Fold in the rhubarb and strawberries with a palette knife until well mixed.

3 Spoon the mixture into the prepared muffin tin, dividing it equally between the 12 holes.

4 To make the topping, combine the butter, flour, brown sugar, linseeds and a pinch of salt in a food processor and process until the mixture has the texture of coarse breadcrumbs. Add the pecan nuts and pulse a few times until the nuts are chopped small. Sprinkle the topping evenly over the muffin mixture.

5 Bake in the preheated oven for 20–25 minutes or until lightly browned on top and a skewer inserted into the centre comes out clean. Remove from the oven and leave to cool in the tin on a wire rack for about 15 minutes, then remove the muffins from the tin. Serve warm or at room temperature.

berry sunrise smoothie

Calories: 259   **Fat:** 4g   **Sat Fat:** 0.7g   **Salt:** Trace   **Carb:** 48g
Cook: No cooking   **Prep:** 5 min

Serves 1

1 banana

55 g/2 oz silken tofu, drained

175 ml/6 fl oz orange juice

200 g/7 oz frozen mixed berries

1 Roughly chop the banana and the tofu into smaller pieces.

2 Place all of the ingredients in a blender on high speed or use a hand-held blender and then process until smooth. Let the smoothie settle for a few seconds and then process again to fully blend.

3 Serve the smoothie immediately in a tall drinking glass.

pumpkin pecan pancakes

Quick & Easy   Vegetarian

Calories: 228   **Fat:** 4.5g   **Sat Fat:** 0.8g   **Salt:** 0.6g   **Carb:** 43.7g
Cook: 10 min   **Prep:** 5 min

Serves 6

140 g/5 oz plain flour

20 g/¾ oz chopped pecan nuts

50 g/1¾ oz soft light brown sugar

2 tsp baking powder

½ tsp cinnamon

¼ tsp salt

1 egg

300 ml/10 fl oz semi-skimmed buttermilk

190 g/6¼ oz peeled and deseeded pumpkin (prepared weight), mashed

1 tsp vanilla extract

1 spray of vegetable oil spray

125 ml/4 fl oz maple syrup, to serve

1 In a medium bowl, combine the flour, pecan nuts, brown sugar, baking powder, cinnamon and salt. In a large bowl, whisk the egg, buttermilk, pumpkin and vanilla extract. Whisk the dry ingredients into the wet ingredients and mix well.

2 Spray a non-stick frying pan with the vegetable oil spray and heat over a medium–high heat. When hot, ladle in the batter 60 ml/2 fl oz at a time to make 8–10-cm/3–4-inch pancakes.

3 Cook for about 2–3 minutes or until bubbles begin to burst in the top and the base is lightly coloured. Flip over and cook for about a further 2 minutes or until the second side is lightly coloured. Serve immediately with maple syrup.

chocolate banana smoothie

Stay Fuller For Longer

Wheat, Gluten & Dairy Free

Vegetarian

Quick & Easy

Calories: 271 **Fat:** 9g **Sat Fat:** 2.5g **Salt:** 0.3g **Carb:** 33.5g
Cook: No cooking **Prep:** 5 min

Serves 1

½ banana

55 g/2 oz silken tofu, drained

160 ml/5½ fl oz reduced-fat soya milk

1 tbsp clear honey

2 tbsp cocoa powder

½ tsp vanilla extract

1 Roughly chop the banana and the tofu into smaller pieces.

2 Combine all of the ingredients in a blender on high speed or use a hand-held blender until well mixed and the cocoa powder has been fully incorporated.

3 Serve the smoothie immediately in a tall drinking glass.

wholemeal crêpes

Calories: 238   Fat: 13g   Sat Fat: 6g   Salt: 0.8g   Carb: 38g
Cook: 20–30 min   Prep: 10 min

Serves 6

Mushroom filling

1 tbsp olive oil

1 garlic clove, finely chopped

1 shallot, finely chopped

675 g/1 lb 8 oz button mushrooms, sliced

½ tsp salt

½ tsp pepper

Crêpes

150 g/5½ oz wholemeal flour

2 large eggs

300 ml/10 fl oz skimmed milk

½ tsp salt

2 tbsp unsalted butter, melted

2 sprays of vegetable oil spray

115 g/4 oz reduced-fat soured cream, to serve

3 tbsp finely chopped chives, to garnish

1 To make the mushroom filling, heat the oil in a large frying pan over a medium–high heat. Add the garlic and shallot and cook for about 5 minutes, stirring occasionally, until soft. Add the mushrooms and continue to cook for about 5 minutes, stirring, until they soften and begin to colour. Season to taste with the salt and pepper. Remove from heat and set aside.

2 To make the crêpes, place the flour, eggs, milk, salt and butter in a medium bowl. Beat together with an electric whisk.

3 Coat a large non-stick frying pan with vegetable oil spray and place it over a medium heat. When the frying pan is hot, ladle the crêpe mixture, about 60 ml/2 fl oz at a time, into the hot frying pan. Tilt the frying pan this way and that to spread the mixture into a thin, even round about 15 cm/6 inches in diameter. Cook for about 1 minute until the crêpe begins to colour lightly underneath. Using a palette knife, gently flip the crêpe over and cook for a further 45 seconds on the other side, or until it is lightly coloured. Stack the crêpes as they are cooked and keep warm.

4 When all of the crêpes are cooked, spoon 2–3 tbsp of the filling onto each crêpe and fold in half twice. Serve with a dollop of soured cream and garnish with finely chopped chives.

breakfast burrito

Vegetarian   Quick & Easy

Calories: 288   **Fat:** 6g   **Sat Fat:** 2.5g   **Salt:** 2.8g   **Carb:** 47g
Cook: 5 min   **Prep:** 5 min

Serves 1

2 egg whites

pinch of salt

¼ tsp pepper

1 spring onion, thinly sliced

1 spray of vegetable oil spray

30 g/1 oz red or green pepper, diced

2 tbsp canned black beans, rinsed

1 wholemeal flour tortilla, warmed

15 g/½ oz crumbled vegetarian feta cheese

2 tbsp salsa

1 tsp finely chopped coriander, plus extra to garnish

1 In a small bowl, combine the egg whites, salt, pepper and spring onion and stir well.

2 Spray a non-stick frying pan with vegetable oil spray and place it over a medium–high heat. Add the red pepper and cook, stirring, for about 3 minutes or until it begins to soften. Reduce the heat to medium, pour in the egg mixture and cook, stirring often, for a further 1–2 minutes or until the egg sets.

3 Put the beans in a microwave-safe bowl and microwave on high for about 1 minute or until heated through.

4 Spoon the cooked egg mixture onto the tortilla. Top with the beans, cheese, salsa and coriander. Serve immediately, garnished with whole coriander leaves.

1

crustless sweetcorn & cheddar quiche

Calories: 298   Fat: 19g   Sat Fat: 10g   Salt: 1.8g   Carb: 14g

Cook: 35–40 min   Prep: 15 min

Serves 6

1 spray of vegetable oil spray

2 tbsp dried breadcrumbs

10 g/¼ oz unsalted butter

½ onion, diced

1 garlic clove, finely chopped

4 eggs

475 ml/16 fl oz skimmed milk

3 spring onions, thinly sliced

1 tbsp plain flour

1 tsp salt

¼ tsp pepper

dash of hot pepper sauce, or to taste

135 g/4¾ oz frozen sweetcorn kernels, thawed

200 g/7 oz mature Cheddar cheese, grated

1 Preheat the oven to 220°C/425°F/Gas Mark 7. Spray a 23-cm/9-inch pie dish with the oil and coat with the breadcrumbs.

2 Melt the butter in a heavy-based frying pan over a medium–high heat. Add the onion and garlic and cook, stirring, for about 5 minutes or until soft. Remove from the heat.

3 In a large bowl, whisk the eggs, milk, spring onions, flour, salt, pepper and hot pepper sauce. Stir in the sweetcorn, sautéed onions and garlic and three quarters of the cheese. Pour the mixture into the prepared pie dish and sprinkle the remaining cheese evenly over the top.

4 Bake in the preheated oven for about 35–40 minutes or until the top is golden brown and the quiche is set in the centre. Remove from oven and set on a rack to cool. Cut into wedges and serve warm or at room temperature.

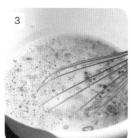

egg white omelette

Vegetarian

Quick & Easy

Calories: 160   **Fat:** 10g   **Sat Fat:** 6g   **Salt:** 0.8g   **Carb:** 4g
Cook: 3–5 min   **Prep:** 15 min

Serves 1

½ red pepper, deseeded

2 large egg whites

1 spring onion, thinly sliced

pinch of salt

pinch of pepper

1 spray of vegetable or olive oil spray

30 g/1 oz fresh vegetarian goat's cheese

2 tsp chopped fresh basil, plus extra to garnish

snipped chives, to garnish

1 Preheat the grill. Put the red pepper on a baking tray under the grill, skin-side up, and roast until it begins to blacken. Remove and place in a polythene bag or a bowl covered with clingfilm and set aside until cool enough to handle. Discard the blackened skin and dice the pepper.

2 In a small bowl, mix the egg whites, spring onion, salt and pepper together, stirring to combine well.

3 Coat a frying pan with the vegetable or olive oil spray and heat over a medium heat. Add the egg mixture and cook for about 3 minutes or until the egg is set, turning the frying pan frequently and running a palette knife around the edge to maintain a thin, even layer of egg.

4 Crumble the goat's cheese in a strip down the centre of the omelette, then top with the diced pepper and the basil. Fold the sides over the filling and slide the omelette onto a plate. Serve immediately, garnished with basil and chives.

poached eggs in tomato sauce

Vegetarian

Calories: 299   **Fat:** 16g   **Sat Fat:** 5g   **Salt:** 1.6g   **Carb:** 21g
Cook: 30–35 min   **Prep:** 10 min

Serves 4

1 tbsp olive oil

1 small onion, diced

2 garlic cloves, finely chopped

½ tsp salt

½ tsp pepper

½ tsp chilli flakes

4 tbsp vegetarian red wine

375 g/13 oz canned chopped tomatoes, with juice

2 tsp finely chopped fresh oregano, thyme, basil, sage or other fresh herb

4 eggs

4 slices toasted wholemeal rustic bread, to serve

2 tbsp finely chopped Kalamata olives, to serve

55 g/2 oz grated vegetarian Parmesan-style cheese, to serve

1 Heat the oil in a large frying pan over a medium–high heat. Add the onion and garlic and cook, stirring occasionally, for about 5 minutes or until soft. Add the salt, pepper, chilli flakes and wine and cook for a further few minutes until the liquid has mostly evaporated. Add the tomatoes and their juice, bring to the boil, then reduce the heat to medium–low and simmer for about 15–20 minutes or until the sauce thickens. Stir in the fresh herbs.

2 Make four wells in the sauce and carefully crack the eggs into them. Cover and cook at a hearty simmer for about 7–9 minutes or until the whites are set but the yolks are still runny.

3 Put the toast slices on four serving plates. Carefully scoop the eggs out of the sauce and place one on each slice of toast. Place spoonfuls of the sauce around the egg and top with a sprinkling of chopped olives and Parmesan-style cheese. Serve immediately.

cheesy sweetcorn muffins

Vegetarian

Calories: 300   Fat: 13g   Sat Fat: 7g   Salt: 0.9g   Carb: 39g
Cook: 30 min   Prep: 10 min

Makes 12

2 sprays of vegetable oil spray

140 g/5 oz plain flour

200 g/7 oz polenta

165 g/5¾ oz sugar

2 tsp baking powder

1 tsp salt

2 eggs

235 ml/8¼ fl oz skimmed milk

135 g/4¾ oz fresh or frozen sweetcorn

115 g/4 oz mild green or jalapeno chillies, chopped

6 tbsp unsalted butter, melted

150 g/5½ oz vegetarian Cheddar cheese, grated

1 Preheat the oven to 180°C/350°F/Gas Mark 4. Spray a 12-hole muffin tin with vegetable oil spray.

2 In a large mixing bowl, combine the flour, polenta, sugar, baking powder and salt. In a medium bowl, beat together the eggs, milk, corn, chillies, butter and half the cheese. Add the wet ingredients to the dry ingredients and mix well.

3 Divide the batter evenly between the muffin holes and sprinkle with the remaining cheese. Bake in the preheated oven for about 30 minutes or until lightly browned on top and a skewer inserted into the centre of one of the muffins comes out clean. Serve warm or at room temperature.

ham & cheese scones

Calories: 265   Fat: 12g   Sat Fat: 7g   Salt: 1.4g   Carb: 31g

Cook: 25 min   Prep: 10 min

Makes 8

290 g/10¼ oz plain flour, plus extra for dusting

2 tsp baking powder

1 tsp sugar

¼ tsp bicarbonate of soda

¼ tsp salt

pinch of pepper

55 g/2 oz unsalted butter, cut into small pieces

300 ml/10 fl oz skimmed buttermilk

115 g/4 oz Cheddar cheese, grated

115 g/4 oz cooked ham, diced

3 spring onions, thinly sliced

1 Preheat the oven to 200°C/400°F/Gas Mark 6. Line a baking tray with baking paper.

2 In a large bowl, combine the flour, baking powder, sugar, bicarbonate of soda, salt and pepper. Add the butter and rub the mixture between your hands until the texture resembles coarse breadcrumbs. Alternatively, pulse the dry ingredients with the butter in a food processor.

3 Add the buttermilk, cheese, ham and spring onions and stir to mix well. The mixture will be fairly sticky. On a lightly floured board, knead the mixture several times with floured hands.

4 Transfer the mixture to the prepared baking sheet and pat it out into a round about 1 cm/½ inch thick and about 23 cm/ 9 inches in diameter. Score into wedges with a sharp knife or pizza cutter.

5 Bake in the preheated oven for about 25 minutes or until golden brown. Cool on a wire rack. Serve the scones warm or at room temperature.

Chapter 2
Lunch

chicken & bacon salad

Quick & Easy

Calories: 300   **Fat:** 18g   **Sat Fat:** 6g   **Salt:** 1.3g   **Carb:** 6.5g

Cook: 15 min   **Prep:** 10 min

Serves 4

Dressing

2 tbsp balsamic vinegar

1 tsp Dijon mustard

2 tbsp olive oil

½ tsp salt

¼ tsp pepper

Salad

2 eggs

1 spray of vegetable oil spray

4 rashers turkey bacon

500 g/1 lb 2 oz cos lettuce, chopped

2 tomatoes, cut into wedges

225 g/8 oz cooked skinless, boneless chicken breast, diced

55 g/2 oz blue cheese, crumbled

1 Whisk all the dressing ingredients in a small bowl until emulsified.

2 Bring a small saucepan of water to the boil. Add the eggs and simmer for about 13 minutes until hard boiled. Remove, put the eggs into ice water and set aside until cool. Peel the eggs, discard the yolks and chop the whites.

3 Spray a non-stick frying pan with vegetable oil and heat it over a medium–high heat. Add the turkey bacon and cook for about 2–3 minutes per side or until lightly coloured and crisp.

4 In a large bowl, combine the lettuce and tomato and toss to mix. Add several spoonfuls of the dressing and toss again to coat. Divide the salad equally between four serving plates. Top each with the chicken, turkey bacon, cheese and chopped egg white. Drizzle with the remaining dressing and serve immediately.

tomato & feta salad

Calories: 265   **Fat:** 17g   **Sat Fat:** 6g   **Salt:** 2.8g   **Carb:** 17g

Cook: No cooking   **Prep:** 10 min

Serves 1

Dressing

1 tbsp red wine vinegar

1 tbsp water

½ tsp Dijon mustard

¼ tsp salt

¼ tsp pepper

2 tsp olive oil

Salad

2 tbsp chickpeas

4 stoned Kalamata olives, diced

½ cucumber, peeled, deseeded and diced

5 small cherry tomatoes, halved

200 g/7 oz cos lettuce, chopped

30 g/1 oz vegetarian feta cheese, crumbled

1 To make the dressing, combine the ingredients in a small bowl or jar with a lid and whisk or shake until emulsified.

2 In a portable container with a lid, layer the salad ingredients, beginning with the dressing. Next add the chickpeas, then the olives, cucumber, tomatoes, lettuce and cheese. Chill upright until ready to serve.

3 To serve, shake the container vigorously to toss the salad. Transfer to a serving plate and serve immediately.

squash & couscous salad

Stay Fuller For Longer

Vegan

Calories: 200   **Fat:** 8.5g   **Sat Fat:** 1.1g   **Salt:** 0.14g   **Carb:** 28g

Cook: 25 min   **Prep:** 25 min

Serves 4

500 g/1 lb 2 oz butternut squash, deseeded, peeled and cut into small chunks

1 onion, roughly chopped

1 garlic clove, crushed (optional)

2 tbsp olive oil

125 g/4½ oz couscous

4 sun-dried tomatoes in oil, drained and chopped

200 ml/7 fl oz boiling water

3 tbsp chopped fresh parsley

1 tbsp lemon juice

salt and pepper

1 Preheat the oven to 200°C/400°F/Gas Mark 6. Place the squash, onion, garlic (if using) and oil in a roasting tin. Toss together. Cover the tin tightly with foil and bake in the preheated oven for 20–25 minutes or until the vegetables are just tender. Leave for 5 minutes before removing the foil.

2 While the vegetables are cooking, place the couscous and sun-dried tomatoes in a heatproof bowl. Pour the boiling water over the couscous, then cover the bowl and leave for about 10 minutes or until all the liquid is absorbed.

3 Fluff up the couscous with a fork. Add the couscous mixture to the vegetables and their juices in the roasting tin with the parsley and lemon juice. Season to taste with salt and pepper, then gently toss together. Serve warm or cold.

prawn taco salad

Quick & Easy

Calories: 286   **Fat:** 8g   **Sat Fat:** 1g   **Salt:** 3.2g   **Carb:** 4g
Cook: 10 min   **Prep:** 15 min

Serves 4

Salad

2 corn tortillas

1 spray of vegetable oil spray

2 tsp salt

450 g/1 lb prawns, peeled and deveined, thawed if frozen

500 g/1 lb 2 oz cos lettuce, chopped

300 g/10½ oz cucumber, sliced

135 g/4¾ oz sweetcorn kernels, thawed if frozen

2 tomatoes, cut into wedges

Dressing

2 tbsp olive oil

2 tbsp lime juice

1 garlic clove, finely chopped

½ tsp ground cumin

½ tsp salt

1 tbsp diced red onion

1 tbsp finely chopped coriander

1 Preheat the oven to 200°C/400°F/Gas Mark 6. Line a large baking tray with foil.

2 Spray the tortillas on both sides with vegetable oil. Cut them in half, then cut the halves into 5-mm/¼-inch wide strips. Put the strips in a single layer on the prepared baking tray and bake for about 10 minutes or until crisp and lightly browned. Remove from the oven and leave to cool on the baking tray.

3 While the tortilla strips bake, put 1 litre/1¾ pints of water and the salt in a large saucepan and bring to the boil over a high heat. Add the prawns, reduce the heat to medium and simmer for about 4 minutes or until the prawns are cooked through. Drain the prawns, put them in a bowl and refrigerate until ready to use.

4 To make the dressing, whisk together the olive oil, lime juice, garlic, cumin and salt until emulsified. Stir in the onion and coriander and mix well.

5 In a large bowl, combine the lettuce, cucumber, sweetcorn and tomatoes and toss well. Add several spoonfuls of the dressing and toss to coat. Divide the salad evenly between four serving plates. Top each with the cooked prawns and drizzle with some of the dressing. Garnish with the tortilla strips and serve immediately.

chicken & spicy peanut salad

Calories: 296   **Fat:** 12g   **Sat Fat:** 2.5g   **Salt:** 0.9g   **Carb:** 16g
Cook: No cooking   **Prep:** 10 min

Serves 4

4 tbsp reduced-fat crunchy peanut butter

2 tbsp lemon juice

1 garlic clove, finely chopped

1 tbsp finely chopped fresh ginger

2 tsp sesame oil

1 tbsp soft light brown sugar

1 tbsp gluten-free tamari (soy sauce)

1 tbsp water

¼–½ tsp cayenne pepper

2 tbsp finely chopped coriander,
plus extra to garnish

2 spring onions, thinly sliced

400 g/14 oz chopped cos lettuce

300 g/10½ oz cucumber, sliced

1 small red, yellow or orange pepper,
deseeded and diced

350 g/12 oz cooked skinless,
boneless chicken breast, diced

1 In a small bowl, combine the peanut butter, lemon juice, garlic, ginger, sesame oil, brown sugar, tamari, water and cayenne. Stir well. Stir in the coriander and spring onions.

2 In a large serving bowl, toss the lettuce, cucumber and pepper. Add a few spoonfuls of the peanut dressing and toss to coat. Divide the salad between four serving plates or bowls. Top with the chicken, then drizzle with more of the dressing. Garnish with finely chopped coriander and serve immediately.

sweet potato soup

Calories: 182   Fat: 8.5g   Sat Fat: 6.5g   Salt: 1g   Carb: 25g
Cook: 30 min   Prep: 5 min

Serves 6

2 tsp vegetable oil

1 onion, diced

1 tbsp finely chopped fresh ginger

1 tbsp vegan gluten-free Thai red curry paste

1 tsp salt

660 g /1 lb 7 oz orange-fleshed sweet potatoes, peeled and diced

400 ml/14 fl oz canned light coconut milk

1 litre/1¾ pints gluten-free vegetable stock

juice of 1 lime

30 g/1 oz finely chopped fresh coriander, to garnish

1 In a large, heavy-based saucepan, heat the oil over a medium–high heat. Add the onion and ginger and cook, stirring, for about 5 minutes or until soft. Add the curry paste and salt and cook, stirring, for a further minute or so. Add the sweet potatoes, coconut milk and vegetable stock and bring to the boil. Reduce the heat to medium and simmer, uncovered, for about 20 minutes or until the sweet potatoes are soft.

2 Purée the soup, either in batches in a blender or food processor or using a hand-held blender. Return the soup to the heat and bring back up to a simmer. Just before serving, stir in the lime juice. Serve hot, garnished with coriander.

roast tomato soup

Vegetarian

Calories: 263 **Fat:** 15g **Sat Fat:** 3.5g **Salt:** 2g **Carb:** 26g
Cook: 1¼ hr **Prep:** 25 min

Serves 4

1.3 kg/3 lb plum tomatoes, halved, stalk ends removed

1 red onion, roughly chopped

6 garlic cloves, peeled

2 tbsp olive oil

½ tsp salt

1 tsp pepper

6 sprigs fresh thyme

1 litre/1¾ pints vegetable stock

2 tbsp lemon juice

Parmesan croûtons

100 g/3½ oz cubed wholemeal bread

2 tbsp olive oil

½ tsp salt

¼ tsp pepper

2 tbsp vegetarian Parmesan-style cheese

1 Preheat the oven to 230°C/450°F/Gas Mark 8. On a large baking tray, toss the tomatoes, onion and garlic with the olive oil, salt, pepper and thyme. Spread the vegetables out into a single layer, arranging the tomatoes cut-side up, and roast in the preheated oven for about 45 minutes or until the vegetables are soft.

2 To make the croûtons, reduce the oven heat to 150°C/300°F/Gas Mark 2. Toss the cubed bread with the olive oil and sprinkle with the salt and pepper. Spread the bread cubes in an even layer on a baking tray and bake in the preheated oven for about 25 minutes. Sprinkle with the cheese, return to the oven and bake for a further 5 minutes or until cheese is melted and beginning to brown.

3 Finish the soup while the croûtons are baking. Purée the vegetables along with the stock, in several batches, in a blender or food processor. Alternatively purée the vegetables and stock in a large saucepan using a hand-held blender.

4 Bring the purée to the boil in a large saucepan over a high heat. Reduce the heat to medium and simmer, stirring occasionally, for about 15 minutes. Just before serving, stir in the lemon juice. Serve hot, garnished with croûtons.

chicken noodle soup

Stay Fuller For Longer

Calories: 292   **Fat:** 3.5g   **Sat Fat:** 0.5g   **Salt:** 1.6g   **Carb:** 31.5g
Cook: 25–30 min   **Prep:** 15 min

Serves 6

1 tbsp olive oil

1 onion, diced

4 garlic cloves, finely chopped

2 carrots, diced

2 celery sticks, diced

1.5 litres/2½ pints chicken stock

4 sprigs fresh thyme

1 bay leaf

1 tsp salt

½ tsp pepper, plus extra to garnish

450 g/1 lb skinless, boneless chicken breasts

225 g/8 oz dried pasta

grated zest and juice of 1 lemon

1 In a large, heavy-based saucepan, heat the olive oil over a medium–high heat. Add the onion and garlic and sauté, stirring frequently, for about 5 minutes or until soft. Add the carrots and celery and cook for a further 1–2 minutes. Add the stock, thyme, bay leaf, salt and pepper and bring to the boil.

2 Reduce heat to medium–low and add the chicken breasts. Simmer for about 20 minutes or until the chicken is cooked through without any signs of pink when the thickest part of the meat is cut through with a sharp knife. Remove the chicken from the pan and set aside. When cool enough to handle, cut the chicken into bite-sized pieces.

3 Remove the thyme sprigs and bay leaf from the soup and discard them. Return the soup to a simmer over a medium heat.

4 Cook the pasta according to the instructions on the packet and drain. Add the cooked pasta and cooked chicken to the soup and simmer for about 5 minutes or until heated through. Just before serving, stir in the lemon zest and juice.

5 Serve immediately, garnished with freshly ground pepper.

chicken tacos

Calories: 300   Fat: 2g   Sat Fat: 0.5g   Salt: 1.6g   Carb: 43.5g
Cook: 15 min   Prep: 20 min

Serves 4

Salsa

½ red onion, diced

2 jalapeno peppers, deseeded and diced

4 tomatoes, diced

10 g/¼ oz coriander, chopped

3 tbsp lime juice

½ tsp salt

Chicken filling

2 tsp soft light brown sugar

2 tsp ground cumin

1 tsp chilli powder

½ tsp salt

½ tsp pepper

400 g/14 oz skinless, boneless chicken breasts

8 small corn tortillas (25 g/1 oz each), to serve

200 g/7 oz lettuce, shredded, to serve

1 Make the salsa by putting the onion, jalapeno peppers and tomatoes into a medium bowl and stirring well. Add the coriander, lime juice and salt and stir to combine.

2 To make the chicken filling, preheat the grill to high or put a griddle pan over high heat. In a small bowl, combine the brown sugar, cumin, chilli powder, salt and pepper. Rub the spice mixture all over the chicken breasts. Grill the chicken breasts over high heat for about 4 minutes per side or until lightly browned on the outside and cooked through with no signs of pink when cut through with a sharp knife. Remove from heat and leave for about 5 minutes, then slice into 5-mm/¼-inch thick slices.

3 To serve, heat the tortillas briefly on the grill, then top with the chicken, salsa and lettuce. Serve immediately.

stuffed aubergines

Vegetarian

Calories: 287 **Fat:** 14g **Sat Fat:** 4.2g **Salt:** 2.1g **Carb:** 29g
Cook: 45 min **Prep:** 15 min

Serves 4

2 medium aubergines (1.25 kg/2 lb 2 oz)

1 tbsp olive oil

1 small onion, diced

2 garlic cloves, finely chopped

135 g/4¾ oz quinoa

350 ml/12 fl oz vegetable stock

1 tsp salt

pinch of pepper

2 tbsp flaked almonds, toasted

3 tbsp finely chopped fresh mint

85 g/3 oz vegetarian feta cheese, crumbled

1 Preheat the oven to 230°C/450°F/Gas Mark 8. Place the aubergines on a baking tray and bake for 15 minutes or until soft. Remove from the oven and leave to cool slightly.

2 Meanwhile, heat the olive oil in a large, heavy-based frying pan over a medium–high heat. Add the onion and garlic and cook, stirring occasionally, for about 5 minutes or until soft. Add the quinoa, stock, salt and pepper.

3 Cut each aubergine in half lengthways and scoop out the flesh, leaving a 5-mm/¼-inch thick border inside the skin so they hold their shape. Chop the flesh and stir it into the quinoa mixture in the frying pan. Reduce the heat to medium–low, cover and cook for about 15 minutes or until the quinoa is cooked through. Remove from the heat and stir in the almonds, 2 tablespoons of the mint and half the cheese.

4 Stuff the quinoa mixture equally among the aubergine skins and top with the remaining cheese. Bake in the oven for about 10–15 minutes or until the cheese is bubbling and beginning to brown. Garnish with the remaining mint and serve.

falafel pitta parcels

Calories: 221 **Fat:** 5g **Sat Fat:** 1g **Salt:** 0.2g **Carb:** 35g
Cook: 10 min **Prep:** 15 min

Serves 4

2 garlic cloves

2 tbsp each of chopped flat-leaf parsley and coriander

1 tsp ground cumin

¼ tsp salt

275 g/9½ oz canned chickpeas, drained and rinsed

2 spring onions, sliced

2 tbsp plain flour

1 tsp baking powder

1 tbsp vegetable oil

Tzatziki sauce

280 g/10 oz cucumber, peeled, deseeded and grated

¼ tsp salt

125 g/4½ oz plain low-fat yogurt

2 tbsp lemon juice

2 tbsp chopped fresh mint leaves

To serve

2 wholemeal pittas, halved and warmed

2 tomatoes, diced

100 g/3½ oz lettuce, shredded

1 To make the falafel patties, chop the garlic in a food processor. Add the parsley, coriander, cumin and salt and process until the herbs are finely chopped. Add the chickpeas, spring onions, flour and baking powder and process until the texture resembles coarse breadcrumbs. Form the falafel mixture into eight patties, about 5 mm/¼-inch thick.

2 To make the sauce, put the grated cucumber on a double layer of kitchen paper and sprinkle with half the salt. Set aside. In a medium bowl, combine the yogurt, the remaining salt, lemon juice and mint and stir to combine. Bundle the cucumber up in the kitchen paper and, holding over the sink, squeeze out the excess juice. Mix the cucumber into the yogurt mixture. Chill until ready to serve.

3 In a heavy-based frying pan, heat the oil over a medium–high heat. When the oil is hot, add the patties and cook for about 3 minutes or until browned on the base. Turn over and cook until browned on the other side. Drain on kitchen paper.

4 To serve, stuff two falafel patties into each pitta half, drizzle with some of the sauce, then add diced tomato and shredded lettuce. Serve immediately.

roast vegetable melts

Vegetarian

Quick & Easy

Calories: 225 **Fat:** 10.5g **Sat Fat:** 5.5g **Salt:** 1.4g **Carb:** 24g
Cook: 20 min **Prep:** 10 min

Serves 4

2 sprays of olive oil spray

1 red pepper, deseeded and cut into strips

1 small aubergine, sliced into 5-mm/¼-inch circles

2 small courgettes, sliced lengthways into 5-mm/¼-inch thick strips

4 garlic cloves, peeled but left whole

¼ tsp pepper

½ tsp salt

4 slices sourdough bread, toasted

115 g/4 oz vegetarian fontina or Emmenthal cheese, thinly sliced

1 Preheat the oven to 230°C/450°F/Gas Mark 8. Spray a large baking tray with olive oil.

2 Arrange the pepper, aubergine, courgettes and whole garlic cloves in a single layer on the prepared baking tray. Spray with more of the olive oil to coat evenly and sprinkle with the pepper. Roast in preheated oven for about 20 minutes until the vegetables soften and begin to colour. Remove the vegetables from the oven, but leave the oven on.

3 In a small bowl, mash the roasted garlic and salt together into a paste. Spread the paste on the toast slices. Top each slice with one quarter of the roasted vegetables. Finally, top each with a layer of cheese.

4 Put the vegetable-topped toasts on the baking tray and return to the preheated oven. Cook for about 4 minutes or until the cheese melts. Serve immediately.

turkey-avocado & blt wrap

Quick & Easy

Calories: 247   **Fat:** 14g   **Sat Fat:** 3g   **Salt:** 2.4g   **Carb:** 4g

Cook: 5–7 min   **Prep:** 5 min

Serves 2

1 spray of vegetable oil spray

4 rashers turkey bacon

2 tbsp reduced-fat mayonnaise

4 large cos lettuce leaves

115 g/4 oz sliced turkey breast

½ tomato, cut into wedges

½ small avocado, sliced

1 Spray a non-stick frying pan with the vegetable oil spray and heat it over a medium–high heat. Add the turkey bacon and cook, turning once, for about 2–3 minutes per side or until lightly coloured and crisp.

2 Spread the mayonnaise down the centre of each lettuce leaf. Lay the turkey breast slices into the lettuce leaves, then the bacon, tomato and avocado, dividing all ingredients equally. Wrap up and serve immediately.

crab salad sandwiches

Quick & Easy

Calories: 300   **Fat:** 10g   **Sat Fat:** 1g   **Salt:** 2.3g   **Carb:** 30.5g
Cook: 2–4 min   **Prep:** 10 min

Serves 4

1 small fennel bulb with leaves

400 g/14 oz crabmeat, picked over

2 tbsp low-fat mayonnaise

2 celery sticks, finely chopped

2 spring onions, thinly sliced

1 tbsp lemon juice

½ tsp salt

8 slices wholemeal bread

1 Remove the leaves from the fennel bulb, then chop and reserve 1 teaspoon of the leaves. Slice the bulb in half lengthways, then carefully cut each half into paper-thin slices and set aside.

2 In a small bowl, combine the crabmeat, mayonnaise, celery, spring onions, fennel leaves, lemon juice and salt. Stir to mix well.

3 Toast the bread. Divide the crab mixture evenly between four slices of the toasted bread. Top with the paper-thin fennel slices and the remaining four slices of bread. Cut each sandwich in half diagonally and serve immediately.

green salad with yogurt dressing

Vegetarian

Quick & Easy

Calories: 109   **Fat:** 7g   **Sat Fat:** 1.5g   **Salt:** 0.2g   **Carb:** 19g
Cook: No cooking   **Prep:** 15 min

Serves 4

½ cucumber, sliced

6 spring onions, chopped

2 tomatoes, sliced

1 yellow pepper, deseeded and cut into strips

2 celery sticks, cut into strips

4 radishes, sliced

85 g/3 oz rocket

1 tbsp chopped fresh mint, to garnish (optional)

Dressing

2 tbsp lemon juice

1 garlic clove, crushed

150 g/5½ oz low-fat natural yogurt

2 tbsp olive oil

salt and pepper

1 To make the salad, gently mix the cucumber, spring onions, tomatoes, yellow pepper strips, celery, radishes and rocket in a large serving bowl.

2 To make the dressing, stir the lemon juice, garlic, natural yogurt and olive oil together in a small bowl until thoroughly combined. Season to taste with salt and pepper.

3 Spoon the dressing over the salad and toss to mix. Garnish the salad with chopped mint (if using) and serve immediately.

Chapter 3
Dinner

fish tacos with avocado salsa

Quick & Easy

Calories: 300   **Fat:** 14g   **Sat Fat:** 1g   **Salt:** 1.3g   **Carb:** 22g
Cook: 5–10 min   **Prep:** 15 min

Serves 4

Salsa

½ red onion, diced

2 jalapeno peppers, deseeded and diced

2 tomatoes, diced

½ avocado, diced

2 tbsp chopped coriander

3 tbsp lime juice

½ tsp salt

Fish

2 tbsp lime juice

1 tbsp olive oil

1 tsp ground cumin

1 tsp chilli powder

½ tsp salt

400 g/14 oz sole fillet

To serve

8 small corn tortillas (25 g/1 oz each)

300 g/10½ oz red cabbage, shredded

1 Put all the salsa ingredients in a medium bowl and stir to mix well.

2 Heat a grill to medium–high or put a griddle pan over a medium–high heat. In a small bowl, combine the lime juice, olive oil, cumin, chilli powder and salt. Brush the mixture on both sides of the fish fillets. Grill the fish over a medium–high heat for about 2–4 minutes per side or until grill marks start to appear and the fish is opaque and cooked through.

3 To serve, warm the tortillas under the grill, then top them with the fish, salsa and shredded cabbage. Serve immediately.

butternut squash & lentil stew

Calories: 234 **Fat:** 8g **Sat Fat:** 0.8g **Salt:** 1.6g **Carb:** 26.5g
Cook: 30 min **Prep:** 10 min

Serves 4

1 tbsp olive oil

1 onion, diced

3 garlic cloves, finely chopped

2 tbsp tomato puree

2 tsp ground cumin

1 tsp ground cinnamon

1 tsp salt

¼ tsp cayenne pepper

450 g/1 lb butternut squash, diced

100 g/3½ oz brown lentils

450 ml/16 fl oz gluten-free vegetable stock

1 tbsp lemon juice

4 tbsp nonfat natural soya yogurt, to garnish

2 tbsp finely chopped coriander, to garnish

2 tbsp flaked almonds, to garnish

1 Heat the oil in a large saucepan over a medium–high heat. Add the onion and garlic and cook, stirring occasionally, for about 5 minutes or until soft.

2 Add the tomato purée, cumin, cinnamon, salt and cayenne and give it a quick stir. Add the squash, lentils and stock and bring to the boil. Reduce the heat to low and simmer, uncovered, stirring occasionally, for about 25 minutes until the squash and lentils are tender.

3 Just before serving, stir in the lemon juice. Serve hot, garnished with a dollop of the yogurt and a sprinkling of the coriander and almonds.

sweet & sour noodles

Vegetarian   Quick & Easy

Calories: 254   **Fat:** 6g   **Sat Fat:** 1.5g   **Salt:** 2.3g   **Carb:** 40g

Cook: 12–15 min   **Prep:** 10 min

Serves 4

140 g/5 oz dried medium egg noodles

2 tsp sunflower oil

1 large red pepper, deseeded and thinly sliced

150 g/5½ oz beansprouts

5 spring onions, thinly sliced

3 tbsp Chinese rice wine or dry sherry

salt

Sauce

3 tbsp light soy sauce

2 tbsp clear honey

2 tbsp tomato puree

2 tsp cornflour

2 tsp sesame oil

125 ml/4 fl oz vegetable stock

1 Bring a large saucepan of lightly salted water to the boil. Add the noodles, bring back to the boil and cook according to the instructions on the packet until tender but still firm to the bite. Drain.

2 To make the sauce, put the soy sauce, honey, tomato purée, cornflour and sesame oil into a small bowl and mix together until smooth, then stir in the stock.

3 Heat the sunflower oil in a large wok or heavy-based frying pan. Add the red pepper and stir-fry for 4 minutes until soft. Add the beansprouts and stir-fry for 1 minute. Add the noodles and spring onions, then pour the wine and sauce over the vegetables and noodles. Toss together over the heat for 1–2 minutes until the sauce is bubbling and thickened and the noodles are heated all the way through. Serve immediately.

white chicken chilli

Wheat, Gluten & Dairy Free

Calories: 219   **Fat:** 5.5g   **Sat Fat:** 1g   **Salt:** 1.1g   **Carb:** 10g
Cook: 35–40 min   **Prep:** 10 min

Serves 6

1 tbsp vegetable oil

1 onion, diced

2 garlic cloves, finely chopped

1 green pepper, deseeded and diced

1 small jalapeno pepper, deseeded and diced

2 tsp chilli powder

2 tsp dried oregano

1 tsp ground cumin

1 tsp salt

500 g/1 lb 2 oz canned cannellini beans, rinsed and drained

750 ml/1¼ pints gluten-free chicken stock

450 g/1 lb cooked chicken breasts, shredded

juice of 1 lime

25 g/1 oz chopped coriander

1 Heat the oil in a large, heavy-based saucepan over a medium–high heat. Add the onion, garlic, pepper and jalapeno and cook, stirring occasionally, for about 5 minutes or until soft. Add the chilli powder, oregano, cumin and salt and cook, stirring, for about a further 30 seconds. Add the beans and stock and bring to the boil. Reduce the heat to medium–low and simmer gently, uncovered, for about 20 minutes.

2 Ladle about half of the bean mixture into a blender or food processor and purée. Return the purée to the pan along with the shredded chicken. Simmer for about 10 minutes or until heated through. Just before serving, stir in the lime juice and coriander. Serve immediately.

spaghetti with bacon-tomato sauce

Stay Fuller For Longer

Calories: 300   **Fat:** 6g   **Sat Fat:** 2g   **Salt:** 1g   **Carb:** 52g
Cook: 25 min   **Prep:** 10 min

Serves 6

55 g/2 oz bacon

1 shallot, diced

2 garlic cloves, finely chopped

4 tbsp red wine

½ tsp salt

½ tsp pepper

800 g/1 lb 12 oz canned chopped tomatoes, with juice

425 g/15 oz wholewheat spaghetti

2 tbsp grated Parmesan cheese

1 Heat a large frying pan over a medium–high heat. Add the bacon and cook for about 3 minutes on each side or until crisp. Drain the rashers on kitchen paper, then crumble and set aside.

2 Remove the excess bacon grease from the frying pan, leaving about 2 teaspoons. Add the shallot and garlic and cook, stirring occasionally, over a medium–high heat for about 5 minutes or until soft. Add the wine, salt and pepper and bring to the boil. Add the cooked bacon along with the tomatoes and their juice and bring to the boil. Reduce the heat to medium and simmer, uncovered, for about 20 minutes.

3 While the sauce simmers, cook the spaghetti in a large saucepan of boiling water according to the instructions on the packet until tender to the bite. Drain.

4 Divide the pasta between six wide pasta bowls, top with the tomato sauce, garnish with the cheese and serve immediately.

roast pork with gingered apples

Wheat, Gluten & Dairy Free

Calories: 220   **Fat:** 4.5g   **Sat Fat:** 1.5g   **Salt:** 0.8g   **Carb:** 25g
Cook: 45 min   **Prep:** 15 min plus marinating

Serves 4

2 garlic cloves

4 tbsp red wine

2 tbsp soft brown sugar

1 tbsp gluten-free tamari (soy sauce)

1 tsp sesame oil

½ tsp ground cinnamon

½ tsp ground cloves

1 star anise pod, broken into pieces

½ tsp pepper

350 g/12 oz pork fillet

steamed green beans, to serve

Gingered apples

4 Bramley apples, chopped

1 tbsp rice vinegar

1 tbsp soft brown sugar

4 tbsp apple juice

1 tbsp fresh ginger, finely chopped

1 In a bowl large enough to hold the pork, combine the garlic, wine, brown sugar, tamari, sesame oil, cinnamon, cloves, star anise and pepper. Add the pork and toss to coat. Cover and refrigerate for at least 2 hours or overnight.

2 Preheat the oven to 190°C/375°F/Gas Mark 5. Heat a non-stick frying pan over a high heat. Remove the pork from the marinade, letting any excess run off into the bowl. Sear the pork, turning occasionally, in the hot frying pan for about 8 minutes or until browned on all sides.

3 Place the meat in an ovenproof dish and drizzle with a few spoonfuls of the marinade. Roast in the preheated oven for 15 minutes. Turn the meat over, drizzle with more of the marinade and continue to roast for about a further 30 minutes or until cooked through (insert a skewer into the centre of the meat and check that there is no pink meat).

4 While the meat is roasting, make the gingered apples. In a saucepan, combine the apples, vinegar, sugar, apple juice and ginger. Cook over a medium–high heat, stirring occasionally, until the liquid begins to boil. Reduce the heat to medium–low and simmer, stirring occasionally, for about 20 minutes or until the apples are soft and the liquid is mostly evaporated.

5 Once the pork has cooked, remove it from the oven and cover the baking dish in a 'tent' of foil. Leave the meat to rest for about 5 minutes. Slice the meat into 5-mm/¼-inch thick slices and serve with a spoonful of the gingered apples alongside and the green beans.

chipotle-lime prawn burgers

Calories: 300 **Fat:** 7.5g **Sat Fat:** 1.1g **Salt:** 3.3g **Carb:** 31g
Cook: 6–8 min **Prep:** 10–15 min

Serves 4

550 g/1 lb 4 oz prawns, peeled and deveined

1 celery stick, finely diced

2 spring onions, finely chopped

2 tbsp finely chopped coriander

1 garlic clove, finely chopped

½ tsp salt

½ tsp ground chipotle

zest and juice of 1 lime

2 tsp olive oil

2 tbsp reduced-fat mayonnaise

4 small wholemeal burger buns, toasted

4 lettuce leaves

1 Process 450 g/1 lb of the prawns in a food processor. Dice the remaining 100 g/4 oz of prawns. In a medium bowl, combine the puréed and diced prawns. Add the celery, spring onions, coriander, garlic, salt, ground chipotle and lime zest and juice and mix well. Form the mixture into four burgers.

2 Heat the oil in a large, non-stick frying pan over a medium–high heat. Add the prawn burgers and cook for about 3–4 minutes or until browned underneath. Flip the burgers over and cook for a further 3–4 minutes or until browned and cooked through.

3 Spread the mayonnaise onto the lower halves of the buns, dividing evenly. Place one prawn burger on the lower half of each bun, then top with a lettuce leaf and the top half of the bun. Serve immediately.

crab cakes

Calories: 225   Fat: 14g   Sat Fat: 2g   Salt: 2.4g   Carb: 9g
Cook: 30 min   Prep: 10 min

Serves 4

Crab cakes

2 sprays of vegetable oil spray

450 g/1 lb crabmeat

1 egg, lightly beaten

1 tbsp reduced-fat mayonnaise

1 tsp Dijon mustard

1 tsp Worcestershire sauce

1 tbsp lemon juice

2 tbsp chopped chives

¼ tsp salt

35 g/1¼ oz dried breadcrumbs

Caper mayonnaise

4 tbsp reduced-fat mayonnaise

2 tsp capers, finely chopped

zest of 1 lemon

1 Preheat the oven to 200°C/400°F/Gas Mark 6. Spray a large baking tray with the vegetable oil spray.

2 In a medium bowl, combine the crabmeat, egg, mayonnaise, mustard, Worcestershire sauce, lemon juice, chives, salt and 25 g/1 oz of the breadcrumbs. Stir to mix well.

3 Put the remaining breadcrumbs on a plate or in a shallow bowl. Form the crab mixture into eight patties about 6 cm/ 2½ inches in diameter and coat them on all sides with breadcrumbs. Put the patties on the prepared baking sheet and spray the tops with vegetable oil spray. Bake in the preheated oven for about 30 minutes or until browned and crisp.

4 Meanwhile, make the mayonnaise. Put all the ingredients into a small bowl and stir to mix well. Serve the crab cakes hot, with a spoonful of caper mayonnaise.

broccoli pizza

Vegetarian

Calories: 274 **Fat:** 9g **Sat Fat:** 4g **Salt:** 1.3g **Carb:** 40.5g

Cook: 18 min **Prep:** 20 min plus rising

Serves 8

240 ml/8¾ fl oz lukewarm water

1¼ tsp easy blend dried yeast

2 tsp salt

1 tsp sugar

1 tbsp olive oil

400 g/14 oz strong white flour, plus extra for dusting

2 sprays of olive oil spray

Topping

150 g/5½ oz small broccoli florets

2 tsp olive oil

1 red onion, thinly sliced

1 garlic clove, finely chopped

1 tbsp chopped fresh oregano

140 g/5 oz vegetarian Emmenthal cheese, grated

¼–½ tsp chilli flakes

1 To make the pizza base, combine the lukewarm water, yeast, salt and sugar in a large mixing bowl and stir well. Leave for about 10 minutes or until bubbly. Stir in the olive oil, then gradually mix in the flour with an electric whisk or food processor until the mixture comes together in a ball. Turn the dough out on to a lightly floured surface and knead, adding a little more flour if needed, for a minute or two or until firm. Wash and dry the mixing bowl, then spray with olive oil. Put the dough in the bowl, cover with clingfilm and leave to rise in a warm place for about an hour, until doubled in size.

2 Preheat the oven to 230°C/450°F/Gas Mark 8. Spray a baking tray with olive oil. Roll out the dough into a large rectangle and place it on the prepared baking tray. Bake in the preheated oven for about 8 minutes or until just beginning to brown.

3 Meanwhile, put the broccoli in a microwave-safe bowl along with 4 tablespoons of water and cover tightly with clingfilm. Microwave on high for about 3 minutes or until the broccoli is just tender. Drain and chop the broccoli into small pieces.

4 Heat the olive oil in a frying pan over a medium heat. Add the onion and garlic. Cook, stirring occasionally, for about 5 minutes or until soft. Remove from the heat and stir in the oregano. Spread the onion mixture evenly onto the part-baked pizza base and top it with the broccoli, then sprinkle with the cheese and chilli flakes. Bake for about 10 minutes or until the cheese is melted, bubbling and golden brown. Slice and serve immediately.

chicken & vegetable enchiladas

Calories: 296 **Fat:** 7.5g **Sat Fat:** 3g **Salt:** 2g **Carb:** 35g

Cook: 50 min **Prep:** 15 min

Serves 4

2 sprays of olive oil spray

2 courgettes, diced

1 red pepper, deseeded and diced

1 tsp salt

1 onion, diced

2 garlic cloves, finely chopped

1 tbsp chilli powder

1 tbsp dried oregano

175 ml/6 fl oz passata

240 ml/8¼ fl oz vegetable stock

175 g/6 oz cooked chicken breast, shredded

8 small corn tortillas (25 g/1 oz each)

75 g/2½ oz reduced-fat Cheddar cheese, grated

1 Preheat the oven to 230°C/450°F/Gas Mark 8. Spray a large, rimmed baking tray with half a spray of olive oil spray.

2 Spread the courgettes and pepper on the prepared baking tray and spray with half a spray of olive oil spray. Sprinkle with half of the salt. Bake in the preheated oven for about 20 minutes or until soft and beginning to brown.

3 Meanwhile, spray a large frying pan with 1 spray of olive oil and place over a medium–high heat. Add the onion and garlic and cook, stirring, for about 5 minutes or until soft. Add the chilli powder and oregano and cook for a further minute. Add the passata and stock and bring to the boil. Reduce the heat to medium and simmer, stirring occasionally, for 5 minutes. Stir in the remaining salt. Purée the sauce, in batches, in a blender or food processor, or use a hand-held blender.

4 When the vegetables are done, remove them from the oven and reduce the heat to 180°/350°F/Gas Mark 4. In a large bowl, combine the vegetables, shredded chicken and several spoonfuls of the sauce. Stir well.

5 Coat the base of a 23 x 33-cm/9 x 13-inch baking dish with a thin layer of the sauce. Place four of the tortillas on the base of the dish, overlapping as little as possible. Top the tortillas with the chicken-vegetable mixture and then a second layer of four tortillas. Top the stacks with the remaining sauce, then sprinkle the cheese over the top.

6 Bake in the preheated oven for about 30 minutes until the enchiladas are heated through and the cheese is bubbling and beginning to colour. Serve immediately.

chicken & sun-dried tomato pasta

Calories: 297   Fat: 4g   Sat Fat: 0.6g   Salt: 1.7g   Carb: 48.2g

Cook: 15–20 min   Prep: 25 min

Serves 6

110 g/3¾ oz sun-dried tomatoes (not packed in oil)

350 g/12 oz boneless, skinless chicken breasts, diced

1 tsp salt

½ tsp pepper

1 spray of vegetable oil spray

2 garlic cloves

40 g/1½ oz fresh basil

1 tbsp olive oil

300 g/10½ oz dried pasta

1 Put the tomatoes in a small bowl and cover with boiling water. Leave to soak for about 20 minutes until soft, then drain, discarding the soaking liquid.

2 Season the chicken with ½ teaspoon of the salt and the pepper. Coat a large, non-stick frying pan with the vegetable oil spray and heat over a medium–high heat. Add the chicken and cook, stirring occasionally, for about 5 minutes or until it is cooked through and just beginning to colour. Set aside.

3 Place the rehydrated tomatoes in a food processor along with the garlic and basil and process to a paste. Add the oil and the remaining salt and continue to process until smooth.

4 Cook the pasta according to the instructions on the packet. Just before draining, scoop out and reserve about 125 ml/4 fl oz of the cooking water. Drain the pasta.

5 Toss the hot pasta with the sun-dried tomato pesto, chicken and as much of the pasta cooking water as needed to make a sauce to coat the pasta. Serve immediately.

halibut with romesco sauce

Quick & Easy

Calories: 261   **Fat:** 7g   **Sat Fat:** 1g   **Salt:** 1.4g   **Carb:** 10g

Cook: 15 min   **Prep:** 10 min

Serves 4

675 g/1 lb 8 oz halibut fillets

¼ tsp salt

½ tsp pepper

Sauce

1 large red pepper

3 garlic cloves, peeled

25 g/1 oz flaked, toasted almonds

1 thick slice of bread, torn into a few pieces

1 tsp salt

1 tsp paprika

250 g/9 oz drained canned chopped tomatoes

2 tbsp red wine vinegar

1 To make the sauce, preheat the grill. Quarter the pepper and place it, cut-side down, on a baking sheet along with the garlic cloves. Grill, turning the garlic once, until the garlic is browned and soft and the skin of the pepper blackens and blisters. Remove from the grill and set aside to cool slightly.

2 When cool enough to handle, peel the blackened skin from the pepper and remove the core and seeds, discarding both. Put the pepper and garlic in a food processor along with the almonds, bread, salt and paprika. Process to a paste. Add the tomatoes and vinegar and process until the tomatoes are smooth and fully incorporated.

3 To cook the fish, preheat a grill to high or heat a griddle pan over high heat. Season the fish with the salt and pepper and grill for about 4 minutes. Turn and grill on the second side for about a further 4 minutes or until the fish is opaque and cooked through. Serve the fish immediately, with the sauce drizzled over it and green vegetables, if liked.

prawn & sausage jambalaya

Calories: 270   Fat: 6g   Sat Fat: 2g   Salt: 1.8g   Carb: 27g
Cook: 40–45 min   Prep: 10 min

Serves 6

1 tbsp olive oil

1 onion, diced

2 garlic cloves, finely chopped

1 green pepper, deseeded and diced

2 celery sticks, diced

160 g/5¾ oz long-grain white rice

1 tbsp paprika

2 tsp dried oregano

2 tsp dried thyme

1 tsp salt

½ tsp cayenne pepper, or to taste

½ tsp pepper

400 g/14 oz canned chopped tomatoes, drained

700 ml/1¼ pints chicken stock

1 bay leaf

450 g/1 lb prawns, peeled, deveined and chopped, thawed if frozen

115 g/4 oz Andouille sausage or spicy Italian sausage, diced

1 Heat the oil in a large, heavy-based saucepan over a medium–high heat. Add the onion, garlic, pepper and celery and cook, stirring occasionally, for about 5 minutes or until soft.

2 Add the rice, paprika, oregano, thyme, salt, cayenne and pepper and cook for about a further 30 seconds. Add the tomatoes, stock and bay leaf. Reduce the heat to medium, cover and cook, stirring occasionally, for about 25–30 minutes or until the rice is tender.

3 Stir in the prawns and sausage and cook, uncovered, for about 6–8 minutes or until the prawns are cooked through. Remove and discard the bay leaf. Serve immediately.

spicy sweetcorn chowder

Calories: 156   **Fat:** 8g   **Sat Fat:** 1g   **Salt:** 0.7g   **Carb:** 20g
Cook: 35 min   **Prep:** 15 min

Serves 6

1 tbsp olive oil

1 onion, diced

2 garlic cloves, finely chopped

2 carrots, diced

2 celery sticks, diced

1 red pepper, deseeded and diced

450 g/1 lb frozen sweetcorn

½ tsp salt

¼ tsp chilli powder

1 litre/1¾ pints gluten-free vegetable stock

225 g/8 oz silken tofu, drained

2 tbsp chopped coriander, to garnish

3 spring onions, thinly sliced, to garnish

1 Heat the oil in a large frying pan over a medium–high heat. Add the onion and garlic and cook, stirring occasionally, for about 5 minutes or until soft. Add the carrots, celery, pepper, sweetcorn, salt, chilli powder and stock. Bring to the boil, reduce the heat to medium–low and simmer, uncovered, for about 20 minutes or until the vegetables are soft.

2 In a blender or food processor, purée the tofu with a ladleful of the soup. Stir the purée into the soup and simmer for about 5 minutes or until heated through. Serve hot, garnished with the coriander and spring onions.

turkey & cranberry burgers

Calories: 247   **Fat:** 3.5g   **Sat Fat:** 0.6g   **Salt:** 0.7g   **Carb:** 69g
Cook: 35 min   **Prep:** 40 min

Serves 4

350 g/12 oz lean ground turkey

1 onion, finely chopped

1 tbsp chopped fresh sage

6 tbsp dry white breadcrumbs

4 tbsp cranberry sauce

1 egg white, lightly beaten

2 tsp sunflower oil, for brushing

salt and pepper

To serve

4 toasted wholemeal burger buns

½ lettuce, shredded

4 tomatoes, sliced

4 tsp cranberry sauce

1 Mix together the turkey, onion, sage, seasoning, breadcrumbs and cranberry sauce in a large bowl, then bind with egg white.

2 Shape into 4 x 10-cm/4-inch burgers, about 2 cm/¾ inch thick. Chill the burgers in the refrigerator for 30 minutes.

3 Preheat the grill to medium and line the grill rack with baking paper, making sure the ends are secured underneath the rack to ensure they don't catch fire. Place the burgers on top and brush lightly with oil. Put under the preheated grill and cook for 10 minutes. Turn the burgers over and brush again with oil. Cook for a further 12–15 minutes or until cooked through.

4 Fill the burger buns with lettuce, tomato and a burger, and top with cranberry sauce.

1

2

4

Chapter 4
Desserts & Snacks

mini pumpkin cheesecakes

Vegetarian

Calories: 290   **Fat:** 13g   **Sat Fat:** 7g   **Salt:** 0.9g   **Carb:** 39g
Cook: 50 min   **Prep:** 15 min plus chilling

Makes 6

2 sprays of vegetable oil spray

115 g/4 oz digestive biscuit crumbs

2 tbsp soft light brown sugar

pinch of salt

1 tbsp unsalted butter, melted

Filling

115 g/4 oz reduced-fat cream cheese

260 g/9½ oz reduced-fat soured cream

250 g/9 oz peeled and deseeded pumpkin (prepared weight), mashed

115 g/4 oz sugar

1 large egg

2 egg whites

½ tsp ground cinnamon

¼ tsp each ground ginger and ground nutmeg

2 tsp vanilla extract

pinch of salt

1 Preheat the oven to 190°C/375°F/Gas Mark 5. To make the base, spray 6 x 125-ml/4-fl-oz ramekins with vegetable oil spray. Pulse the biscuit crumbs, sugar and salt in a food processor several times. Add the butter and pulse until well combined. Press the mixture into the bases and about halfway up the sides of the prepared ramekins. Bake in the preheated oven for 10 minutes until beginning to brown. Remove from the oven and leave to cool slightly. Reduce the oven temperature to 160°C/325°F/Gas Mark 3.

2 To make the filling, beat the cream cheese, soured cream, pumpkin and sugar in a large bowl until smooth. Add the egg and egg whites and continue to beat until well mixed. Add the cinnamon, ginger, nutmeg, vanilla extract and salt and beat well.

3 Spoon the filling into the prepared bases and bake in the preheated oven for about 35–40 minutes or until the cheesecakes are fully set in the middle. Remove and leave to cool to room temperature. Cover and refrigerate for at least 4 hours. Run a knife around the edge of each cheesecake to remove it from the ramekin and serve.

apple-berry crumble

Vegetarian

Calories: 237 **Fat:** 7g **Sat Fat:** 4g **Salt:** 0.4g **Carb:** 34g

Cook: 45 min **Prep:** 10 min

Serves 8

1 spray of vegetable oil spray

6 apples, peeled, cored and sliced

70 g/2 ½ oz dried cranberries or dried cherries

50 g/1¾ oz sugar

½ tsp vanilla extract

Topping

65 g/2¼ oz plain flour

100 g/3½ oz soft light brown sugar

½ tsp ground cinnamon

pinch of salt

55 g/2 oz butter, at room temperature

55 g/2 oz porridge oats

1 Preheat the oven to 190°C/375°F/Gas Mark 5. Spray a baking dish with vegetable oil spray.

2 To make the filling, put the apples, dried fruit, sugar and vanilla extract into a medium bowl and toss to mix thoroughly. Spread the mixture in the prepared baking dish, overlapping the apples a little as necessary.

3 To make the topping, combine the flour, brown sugar, cinnamon and salt in the bowl of a food processor or in a large mixing bowl. In the processor, or using two knives, cut the butter into the flour mixture until it resembles coarse breadcrumbs. Stir in the oats.

4 Sprinkle the topping evenly over the filling and bake in the preheated oven for about 45 minutes or until the topping is crisp and beginning to colour. Serve immediately.

chocolate soufflés

Vegetarian

Calories: 228   Fat: 10g   Sat Fat: 6g   Salt: 0.4g   Carb: 29g

Cook: 25 min   Prep: 15 min

Makes 6

2 sprays of vegetable oil spray

25 g/1 oz unsalted butter

85 g/3 oz plain chocolate, finely chopped

175 ml/6 fl oz skimmed milk

25 g/1 oz cocoa powder

1 tbsp plain flour

1 tsp vanilla extract

pinch of salt

4 egg whites

110 g/3¾ oz sugar

1 Preheat the oven to 190°C/375°F/Gas Mark 5. Spray 6 x 175-ml/6-fl-oz ramekins with vegetable oil spray. Put the butter, chocolate and 60 ml/2 fl oz of the milk in a microwave-safe jug or bowl and microwave on high for 30 seconds. Stir until the chocolate is melted. Add the cocoa powder, flour, vanilla extract and salt and beat until well mixed. Add the remaining milk and stir to combine.

2 In a large bowl, beat the egg whites with an electric whisk on high speed for about 3 minutes or until stiff peaks form. Add the sugar, a little at a time, and continue to beat for about a further 2 minutes or until the mixture is thick and glossy.

3 Gently fold a large dollop of the egg mixture into the chocolate mixture and stir to combine using a palette knife. Gently fold the chocolate mixture into the remaining egg mixture until well combined.

4 Carefully spoon the mixture into the prepared ramekins and bake in the preheated oven for about 22–25 minutes or until the soufflés are puffy and dry on the top. Serve immediately.

pear & blueberry strudel

Vegetarian

Calories: 255   **Fat:** 10g   **Sat Fat:** 4g   **Salt:** 0.4g   **Carb:** 67g
Cook: 40 min   **Prep:** 20 min

Serves 4

25 g/1 oz butter

450 g/1 lb pears, cored and chopped

115 g/4 oz blueberries

1 tbsp soft light brown sugar

½ tsp ground cinnamon

1 slice wholemeal bread, toasted and torn into pieces

1½ tbsp rapeseed oil or sunflower oil

4 sheets of filo pastry

icing sugar, for sprinkling

low-fat custard or low-fat Greek-style yogurt, to serve

1 Melt 1 tablespoon of the butter in a non-stick frying pan. Add the pears and cook over low heat for 5 minutes or until tender. Transfer to a bowl and let cool. Gently stir in the blueberries, sugar and ¼ teaspoon of ground cinnamon.

2 Preheat the oven to 180°C/350°F/Gas Mark 4. Place the toast and the remaining cinnamon in a food processor and blend to coarse crumbs. Melt the remaining butter with the oil.

3 Lay one sheet of filo pastry on a clean work surface and brush lightly with the butter mixture (keep the remaining pastry covered with a damp tea towel while you work to prevent it drying). Sprinkle with one third of the crumbs. Repeat twice more, then cover with the remaining pastry and brush lightly with the butter mixture.

4 Spoon the pear mixture along one long edge and roll up. Press the ends together to seal and transfer to a baking sheet. Brush with the remaining butter mixture and bake in the preheated oven for 40 minutes or until crisp. Sprinkle with a little icing sugar. Serve warm with custard or yogurt.

lemon meringue biscuits

Vegetarian

Calories: 73   **Fat:** 0g   **Sat Fat:** 0g   **Salt:** 0.3g   **Carb:** 18g
Cook: 2 hr   **Prep:** 10 min

Serves 8

2 large egg whites

⅓ tsp cream of tartar

pinch of salt

140 g/5 oz sugar

finely grated zest of 1 lemon

1 Preheat the oven to 110°C/225°F/Gas Mark ¼. Line a large baking tray with foil or baking paper.

2 In a medium bowl, beat the egg whites with an electric whisk on high speed until they are frothy. Add the cream of tartar and salt and continue to beat on high until soft peaks form. Gradually add the sugar and continue to beat on high for about 3–4 minutes or until stiff peaks form. Fold in the lemon zest.

3 Drop the batter in rounded teaspoons onto the prepared baking tray. Bake in the preheated oven for about 1½ hours or until dry and crisp but not yet beginning to colour. Turn off the oven and leave the biscuits inside the oven for a further 30 minutes. Serve at room temperature.

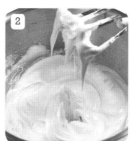

buttermilk brownies

Vegetarian

Calories: 254   **Fat:** 11g   **Sat Fat:** 6g   **Salt:** 0.3g   **Carb:** 38g
Cook: 35 min   **Prep:** 10 min

Makes 8

1 spray of vegetable oil spray

55 g/2 oz plain chocolate, roughly chopped

55 g/2 oz unsalted butter, cut into pieces

225 g/8 oz sugar

40 g/1½ oz cocoa powder

35 g/1¼ oz plain flour

¼ tsp salt

2 eggs

4 tbsp low-fat buttermilk

¼ tsp vanilla extract

1 Preheat the oven to 180°C/350°F/Gas Mark 4. Spray a 20 x 20-cm/8 x 8-inch baking tin with vegetable oil spray.

2 In a microwave-safe dish, combine the chopped chocolate and the butter and heat on high in the microwave for 1 minute. Stir until the chocolate is melted.

3 In a medium bowl, combine the sugar, cocoa powder, flour and salt. In a large bowl, beat the eggs, buttermilk, vanilla and the chocolate-butter mixture until well combined. Add the dry ingredients to the wet ingredients and mix well.

4 Pour the mixture into the prepared baking tin and bake in the preheated oven for about 35 minutes or until the top is dry and a skewer inserted into the centre comes out clean. Cool in the tin on a wire rack. Cut into bars and serve warm or at room temperature.

wholemeal muffins

Stay Fuller For Longer   Vegetarian

Calories: 173   **Fat:** 4.5g   **Sat Fat:** 0.7g   **Salt:** 0.5g   **Carb:** 30g

Cook: 25–30 min   **Prep:** 15 min

Makes 10

225 g/8 oz wholemeal flour

2 tsp baking powder

25 g/1 oz soft light brown sugar

100 g/3½ oz dried apricots, finely chopped

1 banana, mashed with 1 tbsp orange juice

1 tsp finely grated orange rind

300 ml/10 fl oz skimmed milk

1 egg, beaten

3 tbsp rapeseed oil or sunflower oil

2 tbsp porridge oats

fruit spread, honey or maple syrup, to serve

1 Preheat the oven to 200°C/400°F/Gas Mark 6. Place 10 paper muffin cases in a muffin tin. Sift the flour and baking powder into a mixing bowl, adding any husks that remain in the sieve. Stir in the sugar and chopped apricots.

2 Make a well in the centre of the dry ingredients and add the banana, orange rind, milk, beaten egg and oil. Mix together well to form a thick batter. Divide the batter evenly between the 10 paper muffin cases.

3 Sprinkle each muffin with a few porridge oats and bake in the preheated oven for 25–30 minutes or until well risen and firm to the touch. Transfer the muffins to a wire rack to cool slightly. Serve the muffins warm with a little fruit spread, honey or maple syrup.

sweet potato chips

Calories: 202　　**Fat:** 1.5g　　**Sat Fat:** 0.5g　　**Salt:** 0.7g　　**Carb:** 48g

Cook: 15–20 min　　**Prep:** 10 min

Serves 4

2 sprays of vegetable oil spray

900 g/2 lb fleshed sweet potatoes

½ tsp salt

½ tsp ground cumin

½ tsp cayenne pepper

1 Preheat the oven to 230°C/450°F/Gas Mark 8. Spray a large baking tray with vegetable oil spray.

2 Peel the sweet potatoes and slice into 5-mm/¼-inch thick spears about 7.5-cm/3 inches long. Spread the sweet potatoes on the prepared baking tray and spray them with vegetable oil spray.

3 In a small bowl, combine the salt, cumin and cayenne. Sprinkle the spice mixture evenly over the sweet potatoes and then toss to coat.

4 Spread the sweet potatoes out into a single layer and bake in the preheated oven for about 15–20 minutes or until cooked through and lightly coloured. Serve hot.

maple-nut granola bars

Vegan

Calories: 200   **Fat:** 10g   **Sat Fat:** 1.5g   **Salt:** 0.2g   **Carb:** 14.5g

Cook: 5–7 min   **Prep:** 15 min plus chilling

Makes 12

1 spray of vegetable oil spray

165 g/5¾ oz porridge oats

50 g/1¾ oz pecan nuts, chopped

50 g/1¾ oz flaked almonds

120 ml/3¾ ml maple syrup

50 g/1¾ oz soft light brown sugar

60 g/2¼ oz creamy peanut butter

1 tsp vanilla extract

¼ tsp salt

30 g/1 oz puffed rice cereal

30 g/1 oz ground linseeds

1 Preheat the oven to 180°C/350°F/Gas Mark 4. Coat a 23 x 33-cm/9 x 13-inch baking tin with vegetable oil spray.

2 On a large, rimmed baking tray, combine the oats, pecan nuts and almonds and toast in the preheated oven for 5–7 minutes or until lightly browned.

3 Meanwhile, combine the maple syrup, brown sugar and peanut butter in a small saucepan and bring to the boil over a medium heat. Cook, stirring, for about 4–5 minutes or until the mixture thickens slightly. Stir in vanilla extract and salt.

4 When the oats and nuts are toasted, place them in a mixing bowl and add the rice cereal and linseeds. Add the syrup mixture to the oat mixture and stir to combine. Spread the syrup-oat mixture into the prepared baking tin and chill for at least 1 hour before cutting into 12 bars. Store in a tightly covered container at room temperature. Serve at room temperature.

caramel popcorn bites

Vegetarian

Calories: 230   **Fat:** 7.5g   **Sat Fat:** 2.5g   **Salt:** 1.3g   **Carb:** 44g

Cook: 5 min   **Prep:** 1 hour

Serves 8

100 g/3½ oz sugar

110 g/3¾ oz soft light brown sugar

125 ml/4½ fl oz golden syrup

25 g/1 oz butter

1½ tsp bicarbonate of soda

1 tsp salt

½ tsp vanilla extract

80 g/2¾ oz plain, air-popped popcorn

1 Cover a large baking tray with baking paper or kitchen foil.

2 In a saucepan, combine the sugars, golden syrup and butter and bring to the boil over a medium–high heat. Reduce the heat to medium and boil, without stirring, for 4 minutes. Carefully stir in the bicarbonate of soda, salt and vanilla extract.

3 Put the popcorn in a large mixing bowl. Pour the caramel over the popcorn and stir to coat. Using two spoons, form the mixture into 24 balls, about 5 cm/2 inches in diameter, and place them on the lined baking tray. Leave to sit at room temperature for about 1 hour or until firm. Serve at room temperature.

peanut butter biscuits

Vegetarian

Quick & Easy

Calories: 274   **Fat:** 15g   **Sat Fat:** 6.5g   **Salt:** 0.37g   **Carb:** 26.5g
Cook: 14–16 min   **Prep:** 10 min

Serves 12

115 g/4 oz unsalted butter, softened

150 g/5½ oz soft light brown sugar

190 g/6¾ oz reduced-fat peanut butter
(creamy or crunchy)

1 egg

1 tsp vanilla extract

55 g/2 oz porridge oats

70 g/2½ oz plain flour

70 g/2½ oz wholemeal flour

2 tbsp ground linseeds

1 tsp baking powder

1 tsp bicarbonate of soda

½ tsp salt

1 Preheat the oven to 180°C/350°F/Gas Mark 4.

2 In a large bowl, cream the butter and sugar with an electric whisk until smooth. Add the peanut butter, egg and vanilla extract and beat well.

3 In a medium bowl, combine the oats, flours, linseeds, baking powder, bicarbonate of soda and salt. Add the dry ingredients to the wet ingredients and mix well.

4 Drop the batter in rounded tablespoons onto an ungreased baking sheet and flatten slightly with a fork. Bake in the preheated oven for 14–16 minutes or until lightly coloured underneath and around the edges. Leave to cool on the sheet for a few minutes, then transfer to a wire rack to cool completely. Serve warm or at room temperature.

banana split sundae

Vegetarian

Calories: 296   **Fat:** 10g   **Sat Fat:** 4.5g   **Salt:** 0.3g   **Carb:** 49g

Cook: 5 min   **Prep:** 3 hours

Serves 2

2 small bananas

2 tsp flaked almonds, toasted

Chocolate sauce

30 g/1 oz soft light brown sugar

3 tbsp cocoa powder

90 ml/3 fl oz semi-skimmed milk

30 g/1 oz plain chocolate, chopped

½ tsp vanilla extract

1 Peel and dice the bananas, then freeze the diced bananas for 2 hours. In a blender or food processor, process the frozen bananas until creamy. Return the banana purée to the freezer and chill for about 1 hour or until firm.

2 To make the chocolate sauce, put the sugar, cocoa powder and milk in a small saucepan and heat to a simmer over a medium heat. Reduce the heat to low and cook, stirring constantly, for about 1 minute or until the sugar and cocoa powder are dissolved. Remove from the heat and stir in the chopped chocolate until it melts. Stir in the vanilla extract. Leave the sauce to cool slightly.

3 Scoop the banana purée into two bowls, drizzle warm chocolate sauce over the top and sprinkle with the almonds.

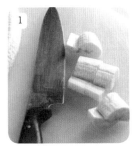

healthy hot chocolate

Vegetarian

Quick & Easy

Calories: 260   **Fat:** 4g   **Sat Fat:** 2g   **Salt:** 0.6g   **Carb:** 48g

Cook: 3 min   **Prep:** 1 min

Serves 1

1 tbsp sugar

2 tbsp cocoa powder

pinch of ground cinnamon (optional)

225 ml/8 fl oz skimmed milk

¼ tsp vanilla extract

1 large marshmallow

1 In a small saucepan, combine the sugar, cocoa powder, cinnamon (if using) and about 2 tablespoons of the milk. Stir to make a paste.

2 Add the remaining milk and heat to a simmer over a medium heat. Cook, stirring occasionally, for about 3 minutes until the cocoa and sugar are completely dissolved.

3 Stir in vanilla extract and serve immediately, topped with a marshmallow.

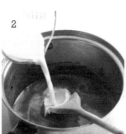